Title

Beyond The Bank Account

Subtitle

Psychological Factors in Financial Struggles"

Author

Abraham Hunter

Copyright

No part of this book may be reproduced, stored,.or transmitted in any form without the prior written permission from the author, except in the case of brief quotations embodied in critical reviews and certain other noncommercial uses permitted by copyright law. The information, opinions, and suggestions presented in this book are solely for informational purposes and should not be

considered as professional advice
The author and publisher disclaim
any liability arising directly
or indirectly from the use or
application of any information
contained in this book.

All rights reserved.© 2024

Introduction

The intricate tapestry of financial struggles, there exists a realm seldom explored but profoundly influential – the realm of psychological factors. While the balance sheet may capture numbers, it is the complex interplay of thoughts, emotions, and behaviors that truly shapes our financial destinies. Welcome to an exploration of the psychological landscape of financial struggles – where the invisible forces wield profound effects on our monetary realities.

In this journey, we delve beyond the mere digits of bank accounts and balance sheets to uncover the deep-rooted beliefs, habits, and biases that silently steer our financial course. Drawing from the wealth of psychological research and real-life narratives, we embark on a quest to unravel the mysteries behind why some thrive while others falter in the realm of finance.

Prepare to confront the invisible barriers that obstruct the path to prosperity – from ingrained attitudes towards money to the psychological toll of financial stress. Through a lens sharpened by insights from behavioral economics, cognitive psychology, and personal finance, we illuminate the shadows cast by self-doubt, impulsivity, and fear.

But this journey is not merely an exercise in diagnosis – it is a call to action, a beacon of hope amidst the shadows. Armed with awareness and understanding, we seek to empower ourselves and others to overcome the psychological barriers that impede financial success. Together, we shall forge a path towards financial resilience, where sound judgment, emotional resilience, and empowered decision-making pave the way to brighter futures.

Join us as we embark on a transformative voyage through the depths of the human psyche and emerge enlightened, emboldened, and equipped to navigate the turbulent waters of financial struggles with clarity, confidence, and resilience.
As we embark on this profound exploration, it is essential to recognize that the journey towards financial stability and prosperity is not merely a matter of dollars and cents. It is a journey of

self-discovery, introspection, and transformation – a journey that transcends the material realm to delve into the recesses of our minds and hearts.

At the heart of every financial decision lies a complex web of psychological factors – beliefs inherited from childhood, fears ingrained by past experiences, and aspirations shaped by societal influences. These psychological forces, often invisible to the naked eye, exert a profound influence on our financial behaviors, shaping the trajectory of our financial lives in ways both subtle and profound.

Consider, for instance, the role of self-esteem in financial decision-making. Research has shown that individuals with low self-esteem may be more prone to impulsive spending, seeking temporary relief or validation through material possessions. Conversely, those with high self-esteem may approach financial decisions with greater confidence and clarity, setting and pursuing long-term goals with determination and resilience.

Moreover, the impact of cognitive biases on financial behavior cannot be overstated. From the overconfidence bias that leads us to overestimate our abilities and underestimate risks, to the confirmation bias that blinds us to alternative viewpoints and evidence, these cognitive shortcuts can distort our perceptions and lead us astray in the realm of finance.

Yet, perhaps most insidious of all is the specter of financial stress – a silent epidemic that afflicts millions, silently eroding mental health, well-being, and productivity. The weight of financial worries can cast a long shadow over every aspect of our lives, sapping our energy, clouding our judgment, and undermining our capacity to pursue our goals and aspirations.

In this intricate dance between the mind and money, it becomes clear that addressing financial struggles requires more than just practical solutions or quick fixes. It demands a holistic approach that acknowledges the interplay of psychological, emotional, and behavioral factors in shaping our financial realities.

Throughout this exploration, we shall draw upon the wisdom of scholars, practitioners, and individuals who have traversed the tumultuous terrain of financial struggles. Through their insights and experiences, we shall illuminate the hidden forces that drive our financial behaviors and chart a course towards greater self-awareness, empowerment, and financial well-being.

So let us embark on this journey with open minds and open hearts, ready to confront the shadows that lurk within and emerge stronger, wiser, and more resilient in our pursuit of financial freedom and fulfillment.

Table of Contents

Title--------------------1

Subtitle----------------2

Copyright--------------3

Introduction-----------5

Chapter One----------16

Chapter Two----------21

Chapter Three--------27

ChapterFour---------33

Chapter Five---------39

Chapter Six----------46

Chapter Seven------53

ChapterEigth--------60

Chapter Nine--------67

Chapter Ten---------74

Chapter Eleven------82

Chapter Twelve-----90

ChapThirteen-------97

Summary-----------105

Chapter:One

Procrastination

Procrastination is the act of delaying or postponing tasks or activities, often despite knowing that doing so could have negative consequences. It's a common behavior that many people struggle with, and it can stem from various factors such as fear of failure, lack of motivation, or poor time management skills. Here are some key points about procrastination:

1. Psychological Factors: Procrastination can be influenced by various psychological factors such as fear of failure, perfectionism, lack of motivation, or difficulty with self-regulation.

2. Temporal Discounting : People tend to prioritize immediate rewards over long-term benefits, leading to procrastination on tasks with delayed rewards.

3. Behavioral Patterns: Procrastination can become a habitual behavior, reinforced by short-term relief from avoiding tasks and a temporary reduction in anxiety.

4. Impact on Performance: Procrastination can lead to decreased productivity, increased stress, missed deadlines, and lower quality work.

5. Factors Influencing Procrastination: Environmental factors like distractions, lack of structure, or unclear goals can contribute to procrastination. Additionally, individual differences such as personality traits and coping strategies play a role.

6. Strategies to Overcome Procrastination: Effective strategies include breaking tasks into smaller,

manageable steps, setting deadlines, creating a supportive environment, practicing time management techniques, and addressing underlying psychological barriers.

7. Mindfulness and Self-Compassion: Cultivating mindfulness and self-compassion can help individuals become more aware of their procrastination habits and develop healthier approaches to task management.

Understanding the root causes of procrastination and implementing strategies to overcome it can lead to increased productivity, improved well-being, and a greater sense of accomplishment.

Chapter Two: The Fear Of Failure

The fear of failure can have various outcomes, affecting individuals emotionally, psychologically, and behaviorally. Here's a detailed breakdown of potential outcomes, step by step:

1. Emotional Impact:

Anxiety: Fear of failure often manifests as anxiety, causing individuals to feel tense, worried, or apprehensive about taking risks or attempting new tasks.

Stress: Persistent fear of failure can lead to chronic stress, as individuals constantly feel pressured to perform well and avoid making mistakes.

- **Low Self-Esteem**: Experiencing failure or fearing failure can erode self-esteem and self-confidence, leading individuals to doubt their abilities and worth.

2. Psychological Effects:
   - Perfectionism: Fear of failure may fuel perfectionistic tendencies,

where individuals set unrealistically high standards for themselves and are overly critical of their performance.

  - Avoidance Behavior: Individuals may engage in avoidance behavior to escape the possibility of failure, procrastinating on tasks or avoiding challenges altogether.

  - Imposter Syndrome: Fear of failure can contribute to imposter syndrome, where individuals doubt their accomplishments and fear being exposed as frauds despite evidence of competence.

3. Behavioral Consequences:
   - Risk Aversion: Fear of failure can make individuals reluctant to

take risks or pursue opportunities for fear of experiencing setbacks or rejection.

- Underachievement: Avoidance of challenging tasks or opportunities for growth can lead to underachievement, as individuals settle for mediocrity rather than striving for excellence.

- Self-Sabotage: Subconscious beliefs about unworthiness or incompetence may lead individuals to engage in self-sabotaging behaviors that undermine their success.

4.Interpersonal Effects:
- Avoidance of Feedback: Fear of failure may lead individuals to

avoid seeking feedback or constructive criticism, fearing it will confirm their inadequacy.

- Strained Relationships: Perfectionism and avoidance behavior can strain relationships, as individuals may withdraw socially or become defensive in response to perceived criticism.

5. Professional Consequences:
 - Career Stagnation: Fear of failure can hinder career advancement, as individuals may shy away from challenging projects or opportunities for growth. - Missed Opportunities: Avoiding risks can result in missed opportunities for

learning, innovation, and personal development.

- Job Dissatisfaction: Chronic fear of failure can lead to dissatisfaction in the workplace, as individuals may feel unfulfilled or stagnant in their careers.

Addressing fear of failure often involves cultivating resilience, challenging negative beliefs, setting realistic goals, and embracing a growth mindset that views failure as an opportunity for learning and growth. Therapy, coaching, and self-help techniques can also be valuable in overcoming the paralyzing effects of fear of failure.

Chapter Three: Relying Solely On One Source Of Income

Relying solely on one source of income can have various outcomes, impacting individuals financially, emotionally, and practically. Here's a detailed breakdown of potential outcomes, step by step:

1. Financial Instability:

- Vulnerability to Economic Changes: Depending on a single income source leaves individuals vulnerable to economic downturns, industry-specific fluctuations, or changes in employer policies.
- Limited Earning Potential: Relying on one source of income may limit overall earning potential, as individuals may miss out on opportunities for additional income streams or career advancement.

2. Emotional Stress:
- Anxiety and Uncertainty: The precariousness of relying on one income source can lead to anxiety and uncertainty about financial stability, especially in times of

unexpected expenses or emergencies.

- Fear of Job Loss: Individuals may experience heightened fear of job loss, as the loss of their sole income source could have significant consequences for their financial well-being.

3. Practical Challenges:
- Limited Flexibility: Having only one income source may limit individuals' flexibility in pursuing personal or professional goals, as they may feel constrained by the need to maintain their primary source of income.
- Difficulty Saving or Investing: With only one source of income,

individuals may find it challenging to save for the future or invest in long-term financial goals such as retirement or education.

4. Dependency on Employer or Industry:

- Lack of Control: Relying on one employer or industry for income leaves individuals with limited control over their financial future, as their income is dependent on external factors beyond their control.

 - Exposure to Risk: Changes in the employer's financial health, management decisions, or market conditions can pose significant risks to individuals relying solely on that source of income.

5. Impact on Lifestyle:
 - Restricted Lifestyle Choices: Depending on one income source may limit individuals' ability to afford certain lifestyle choices, such as travel, leisure activities, or investments in personal development.
- Difficulty Achieving Financial Goals: Limited income may hinder individuals' ability to achieve financial goals such as homeownership, higher education, or starting a business.

6. Family and Relationship Dynamics:

- Strain on Relationships: Financial stress resulting from reliance on one income source can strain relationships, leading to conflicts over money management, spending habits, and future plans.
- Unequal Burden   If one partner is the sole breadwinner, it can create an unequal burden on that individual and affect power dynamics within the relationship.

To mitigate the risks associated with relying solely on one income source, individuals can consider diversifying their income through additional streams such as freelance work, part-time employment, investments, or entrepreneurship. Creating an emergency fund, developing new skills, and networking within their industry can also provide a safety net and increase financial resilience.

Chapter Four:
Lezines

Here's a detailed breakdown of potential outcomes step by step:

1. Decreased Productivity:
 - Incomplete Tasks: Laziness can lead to tasks being left unfinished or completed inadequately,

reducing overall productivity and efficiency.

- Missed Deadlines: Procrastination due to laziness can result in missed deadlines, affecting work performance and reputation.

2. Impact on Personal Goals:
- Stagnation: Laziness can hinder progress towards personal or professional goals, leading to a sense of stagnation and unfulfillment.
- Limited Growth: Failure to take action or pursue opportunities due to laziness can limit personal and professional growth potential.

3. Strained Relationships:
 - Unreliability: Laziness may lead to unreliable behavior, causing strain on relationships as others may feel let down or frustrated by unfulfilled commitments.
 - Resentment: Dependence on others to pick up the slack due to laziness can breed resentment and conflict within personal and professional relationships.

4. Financial Consequences**:
 - **Missed Opportunities**: Laziness can result in missed opportunities for career

advancement, promotions, or additional income streams.

  - **Financial Instability**: Lack of ambition or drive due to laziness can lead to financial instability or reliance on others for financial support.

5. **Health Effects**:
  - **Sedentary Lifestyle**: Laziness often correlates with a sedentary lifestyle, increasing the risk of obesity, cardiovascular disease, and other health issues.
  - **Mental Health**: Chronic laziness can contribute to feelings of apathy, low self-esteem, and

depression, impacting overall well-being.

6. **Impact on Reputation**:
   - **Perception by Others**: Consistently exhibiting lazy behavior can result in a negative perception by peers, colleagues, and employers, potentially damaging one's reputation and opportunities for advancement.
   - **Professional Reputation**: Laziness in the workplace can undermine professionalism and trust, affecting career prospects and future opportunities.

7. **Cyclical Behavior**:

- **Self-Reinforcing Patterns**: Laziness can become a self-reinforcing cycle, where past instances of procrastination and inactivity reinforce future behavior, making it increasingly difficult to break the cycle.

To address laziness, individuals can implement strategies such as setting specific goals, breaking tasks into manageable steps, establishing routines, seeking accountability from others, addressing underlying causes such as lack of motivation or burnout, and cultivating habits of discipline and self-motivation. Seeking support from mentors, coaches, or mental health professionals can also be beneficial in overcoming laziness and fostering personal growth and development.

Chapter Five: Substance abuse

Direct Costs of Substance Abuse:
- **Cost of Purchasing Drugs**: Individuals with substance abuse issues often spend significant amounts of money on purchasing

drugs, which can quickly deplete their financial resources.

   - **Increased Tolerance**: Over time, individuals may develop tolerance to drugs, requiring larger doses to achieve the desired effects, leading to higher expenses.

2. **Indirect Costs and Financial Consequences**:
   - **Healthcare Expenses**: Drug abuse often results in health complications, leading to increased healthcare costs associated with medical treatments, hospitalizations, rehabilitation programs, and therapy.
   - **Legal Expenses**: Involvement in illegal drug activities

can result in legal consequences, including fines, legal fees, and costs associated with legal representation.

- **Lost Income**: Drug abuse can impair cognitive function, decrease productivity, and lead to absenteeism or job loss, resulting in lost income and diminished earning potential.
- **Property Damage and Theft**: Individuals may resort to theft or other criminal activities to fund their drug habits, leading to property damage, legal penalties, and financial restitution.
- **Financial Dependence**: Substance abuse can strain

personal relationships and lead to financial dependence on family members or friends for support, placing additional financial burdens on others.

3. **Long-Term Financial Impact**:
   - **Debt Accumulation**: Excessive spending on drugs and associated expenses can lead to the accumulation of debt, including credit card debt, payday loans, or loans from family and friends.
   - **Impaired Financial Planning**: Drug abuse can impair judgment and decision-making abilities, hindering individuals' ability to effectively manage finances, plan

for the future, and prioritize financial goals.

   - **Asset Depletion**: Individuals may liquidate assets, such as savings accounts, retirement funds, or valuable possessions, to finance their drug habits or cover associated expenses, depleting their financial resources over time.

4. **Interference with Financial Stability and Security**:

   - **Inability to Build Savings**: Drug abuse can prevent individuals from building savings or emergency funds, leaving them financially vulnerable to unexpected expenses or economic downturns.

- **Limited Employment Opportunities**: Substance abuse can negatively impact employability, as individuals may struggle to maintain steady employment, advance in their careers, or pass drug screenings required for certain jobs.

- **Undermined Financial Goals**: Drug abuse can derail individuals' financial goals, such as homeownership, higher education, or retirement planning, as financial resources are diverted towards supporting drug habits.

Addressing drug abuse often requires comprehensive intervention strategies, including seeking professional help through addiction treatment programs, therapy, support groups, and medication-assisted treatment. Developing healthy coping mechanisms, improving financial literacy, and rebuilding relationships are also essential components of recovery and regaining financial stability.

Chapter Six; Gambling

1. **Initial Excitement and Thrill**:
   - **Initial Wins**: Gambling often begins with occasional wins, leading to feelings of excitement, euphoria, and anticipation of more significant winnings.
   - **Perceived Control**: Early success in gambling can create a false sense of control, leading individuals to believe they can

predict or influence future outcomes.

2. **Escalation and Increased Risk-Taking**:
   - **Chasing Losses**: Following initial wins, individuals may experience losses and become motivated to chase their losses by increasing their bets or playing more frequently in an attempt to recoup their losses.
   - **Binge Gambling**: As the thrill of gambling intensifies, individuals may engage in binge gambling sessions, spending extended periods of time at casinos or online gambling sites.

3. **Financial Consequences**:
   - **Loss of Money**: Continuous gambling often results in significant financial losses, as individuals wager more money than they can afford to lose or spend their savings, assets, or borrowed funds in pursuit of gambling wins.
   - **Debt Accumulation**: Gambling addiction can lead to the accumulation of debt, including credit card debt, personal loans, or loans from family and friends, as individuals attempt to finance their gambling habits or cover financial losses.
   - **Financial Instability**: The financial consequences of

gambling can lead to financial instability, strained relationships, bankruptcy, foreclosure, or other adverse financial outcomes.

4. **Psychological Impact**:
   - **Stress and Anxiety**: Gambling addiction can lead to stress, anxiety, and other mental health issues as individuals experience guilt, shame, or regret over their gambling behavior and financial losses.
   - **Depression**: Chronic gambling addiction can contribute to depression, hopelessness, and feelings of despair, particularly as individuals struggle to cope with financial difficulties and

interpersonal conflicts resulting from their gambling behavior.

5. **Social and Interpersonal Consequences**:
   - **Relationship Strain**: Gambling addiction can strain personal relationships, marriages, and familial bonds, as individuals prioritize gambling over spending time with loved ones or fulfilling their social responsibilities.
   - **Isolation**: Individuals may withdraw from social activities and isolate themselves from family and friends to conceal their gambling behavior or avoid judgment and criticism.

- **Legal and Ethical Issues**: Involvement in illegal gambling activities or engaging in deceitful or unethical behavior to finance gambling can result in legal consequences, further exacerbating social and financial problems.

6. **Impact on Work and Career**:
   - **Decreased Productivity**: Gambling addiction can lead to decreased productivity, absenteeism, or job loss as individuals prioritize gambling over work responsibilities or struggle to concentrate due to financial worries or preoccupation with gambling.

- **Professional Consequences**: Gambling addiction can have professional consequences, including disciplinary actions, termination of employment, or difficulties obtaining new employment opportunities due to a tarnished reputation or criminal record resulting from gambling-related offenses.

Addressing gambling addiction often requires professional help, including therapy, support groups, medication-assisted treatment, and financial counseling. Developing healthy coping mechanisms, managing financial stressors, and rebuilding relationships are crucial aspects of recovery from gambling addiction and regaining financial stability and well-being.

Chapter Seven: Reckless Spending:

reckless behavior in the financial aspect:

1. **Impulsive Spending**:
   - **Spending Beyond Means**: Reckless behavior often involves impulsive spending, where individuals regularly exceed their income or budget limits to purchase non-essential items or indulge in extravagant experiences.

- **High Credit Card Balances**: Impulsive spending can lead to high credit card balances, as individuals rely on credit to finance their purchases without considering the long-term consequences of accumulating debt.

2. **Lack of Financial Planning**:
  - **Absence of Budgeting**: Reckless behavior often involves a lack of financial planning, where individuals fail to create or adhere to a budget, track expenses, or prioritize financial goals.
  - **Failure to Save**: Individuals engaging in reckless behavior may neglect to save money for emergencies, future goals, or

retirement, leaving them vulnerable to financial crises or unable to achieve long-term financial stability.

3. **Debt Accumulation**:
   - **Credit Card Debt**: Reckless spending can result in the accumulation of credit card debt, with individuals carrying balances from month to month and paying high interest rates on their outstanding balances.
   - **Loan Defaults**: Failure to manage debt responsibly can lead to defaults on loans, including personal loans, auto loans, or mortgages, resulting in adverse consequences such as damaged

credit, repossession, or foreclosure.

4. **Financial Instability**:
   - **Living Paycheck to Paycheck**: Reckless behavior often leads to financial instability, where individuals struggle to cover basic living expenses and rely on each paycheck to meet immediate financial needs without building savings or planning for the future.
   - **Risk of Bankruptcy**: Persistent financial irresponsibility can increase the risk of bankruptcy, as individuals may reach a point where they are unable to repay their debts or sustain their lifestyle without drastic intervention.

5. **Relationship Strain**:
   - **Conflict Over Finances**: Reckless behavior in finances can strain personal relationships, marriages, and familial bonds, as partners or family members may disagree on spending priorities, financial goals, or allocation of resources.
   - **Trust Issues**: Financial irresponsibility can erode trust in relationships, as partners may feel betrayed or resentful towards individuals who engage in reckless behavior, conceal financial problems, or prioritize their own desires over shared financial goals.

6. **Professional Consequences**:
   - **Career Limitations**: Reckless behavior in finances can have professional consequences, including limitations on career advancement, job loss, or difficulties obtaining new employment opportunities due to a tarnished reputation or poor credit history.
   - **Workplace Stress**: Financial stress resulting from reckless behavior can spill over into the workplace, affecting job performance, concentration, and interpersonal relationships with colleagues or supervisors.

Addressing reckless behavior in finances often requires a combination of self-awareness, financial education, behavior modification, and professional guidance. Developing a budget, practicing mindful spending habits, seeking debt counseling, and addressing underlying psychological factors contributing to reckless behavior are essential steps towards achieving financial stability and well-being.

Chapter Eight:

Womanizing

womanizing in the financial aspect:

1. **Spending on Relationships**:
   - **Extravagant Dates and Gifts**: Womanizing behavior often involves spending significant amounts of money on dates, gifts,

and entertainment to impress or maintain relationships with multiple partners.

   - **Dining Out and Entertainment**: Womanizers may frequently dine out at expensive restaurants, attend lavish events, or engage in costly leisure activities as part of their pursuit of romantic or sexual encounters.

2. **Legal and Financial Obligations**:
   - **Child Support**: Womanizing behavior can result in legal and financial obligations, such as child support payments, if individuals father children out of wedlock or through extramarital affairs.

- **Alimony or Settlements**: Individuals involved in womanizing may face financial consequences in divorce settlements or alimony payments if their behavior contributes to the breakdown of marriages or committed relationships.

3. **Healthcare Expenses**:
   - **STI Testing and Treatment**: Womanizing behavior increases the risk of sexually transmitted infections (STIs), requiring individuals to undergo regular testing and potentially incur expenses for STI treatment or medication.

- **Unplanned Pregnancies**: Womanizing can lead to unintended pregnancies, resulting in medical expenses related to prenatal care, childbirth, and child support obligations if paternity is established.

4. **Impact on Career and Professional Reputation**:
   - **Workplace Distractions**: Womanizing behavior may lead to distractions in the workplace, as individuals spend time and energy pursuing romantic or sexual encounters rather than focusing on job responsibilities.
   - **Damage to Professional Reputation**: Womanizing can

damage professional reputation and credibility, particularly if relationships or encounters with coworkers, clients, or superiors lead to conflicts of interest, harassment allegations, or breaches of workplace policies.

5. **Financial Instability**:
   - **Divorce Costs**: Womanizing behavior can contribute to divorce or relationship breakdowns, resulting in legal fees, asset division, and financial settlements that impact individuals' financial stability and assets.
   - **Diminished Earning Potential**: Legal and financial consequences of womanizing,

such as divorce settlements, child support payments, or damage to professional reputation, can diminish individuals' earning potential and career advancement opportunities.

6. **Emotional and Psychological Impact**:

   - **Stress and Anxiety**: Juggling multiple relationships or encounters can lead to emotional stress, anxiety, and guilt, particularly if individuals struggle to maintain honesty and transparency with partners or experience feelings of emptiness or dissatisfaction.

   - **Relationship Strain**: Womanizing behavior can strain

personal relationships, marriages, and familial bonds, as partners or family members may feel betrayed, neglected, or insecure due to infidelity or lack of commitment.

Addressing womanizing behavior often requires self-reflection, introspection, and accountability, as well as seeking support from mental health professionals, relationship counselors, or support groups. Developing healthy relationship habits, practicing empathy and respect for partners, and addressing underlying emotional needs or insecurities are crucial steps towards personal growth, self-awareness, and building fulfilling and sustainable relationships.

Chapter Nine:

Trying To Pleased Other

Here's a detailed breakdown of potential outcomes, of trying to please others.

1. **Excessive Spending**:
   - **Overspending on Gifts and Treats**: Trying to please others financially often involves spending

money on gifts, treats, or experiences to gain approval or maintain relationships.

   - **Impulse Purchases**: Individuals may make impulsive purchases to impress or please others, even if it means exceeding their budget or financial means.

2. **Financial Obligations**:
   - **Loans and Borrowing**: Trying to please others financially can lead individuals to lend money to friends or family members, or cosign loans, without considering the potential risks or consequences.
   - **Financial Support**: Individuals may feel obligated to

provide financial support to others, such as adult children, aging parents, or needy friends, even if it compromises their own financial stability.

3. **Limited Savings and Investments**:

   - **Neglecting Personal Financial Goals**: Prioritizing others' financial needs or desires over one's own can result in neglecting personal financial goals, such as saving for emergencies, retirement, or major purchases.
   - **Underfunded Retirement Accounts**: Individuals may sacrifice contributions to retirement accounts or investment portfolios to

meet immediate financial demands or expectations from others, jeopardizing their long-term financial security.

4. **Financial Stress and Anxiety**:
   - **Strain on Budget**: Trying to please others financially can lead to stress and anxiety as individuals struggle to balance competing financial priorities, such as paying bills, meeting loan obligations, and satisfying others' expectations.
   - **Debt Accumulation**: Overextending financially to please others can result in debt accumulation, as individuals may rely on credit cards, loans, or lines

of credit to cover expenses or maintain appearances.

5. **Career and Professional Impact**:
   - **Career Sacrifices**: Individuals may make career sacrifices, such as working longer hours, accepting lower-paying jobs, or passing up promotions or career opportunities, to accommodate others' financial needs or preferences.
   - **Professional Stagnation**: Prioritizing others' financial needs over personal advancement can lead to professional stagnation and limited career growth, as individuals may be reluctant to

invest in education, training, or networking opportunities.

6. **Interpersonal Relationships**:
   - **Resentment and Conflict**: Trying to please others financially can lead to resentment and conflict in relationships, particularly if individuals feel taken advantage of or unappreciated for their efforts.
   - **Dependency**: Enabling others financially can foster dependency and perpetuate unhealthy dynamics in relationships, as individuals may become reliant on others' support or contributions.

Addressing the tendency to please others financially requires setting boundaries, practicing assertiveness, and prioritizing one's own financial well-being. Open communication, setting realistic expectations, and finding a balance between generosity and self-care are essential for maintaining healthy relationships and financial stability. Seeking guidance from financial advisors or counselors can also help individuals develop strategies for managing financial obligations while maintaining personal financial goals and boundaries.

Chapter Ten:

Lack Of Mentorship

Here's a detailed breakdown of potential outcomes of the lack of mentorship in the financial aspect:

1. **Limited Knowledge and Skills**:

- **Lack of Guidance**: Without mentorship, individuals may lack access to valuable insights, knowledge, and skills related to financial management, investing, and wealth-building strategies.

- **Missed Learning Opportunities**: The absence of mentorship deprives individuals of opportunities to learn from the experiences, mistakes, and successes of others in the financial realm.

2. **Risk of Making Costly Mistakes**:

- **Trial and Error**: Without mentorship, individuals may resort to trial-and-error approaches in financial decision-making, leading to costly mistakes, missed opportunities, and setbacks.

  - **Exposure to Scams and Fraud**: Lack of guidance increases the risk of falling victim to financial scams, fraudulent schemes, or predatory practices targeting inexperienced individuals.

3. **Limited Networking and Connections**:

  - **Restricted Access to Opportunities**: Mentorship often provides access to valuable networks, connections, and opportunities in the financial industry, including job prospects, investment opportunities, and partnerships.

   - **Missed Collaborative Ventures**: Without mentorship, individuals may miss out on collaborative ventures, partnerships, or joint investments that could accelerate their financial growth and success.

4. **Delayed Career Advancement**:

   - **Stagnation in Career Growth**: Lack of mentorship can hinder career advancement and professional development, as individuals may lack guidance on navigating career paths, negotiating salaries, or seizing growth opportunities.

  - **Limited Feedback and Guidance**: Without mentorship, individuals may struggle to receive constructive feedback, guidance, or mentorship necessary for honing skills, developing expertise, and advancing in their careers.

5. **Emotional and Psychological Impact**:
  - **Feelings of Isolation**: The absence of mentorship may lead to feelings of isolation, insecurity, and self-doubt as individuals navigate financial challenges and uncertainties alone.

- **Stress and Anxiety**: Without mentorship, individuals may experience heightened stress and anxiety related to financial decision-making, as they lack a trusted advisor or sounding board to provide support and guidance.

6. **Missed Opportunities for Personal Growth**:
   - **Limited Personal Development**: Mentorship fosters personal growth, self-awareness, and confidence by providing guidance, encouragement, and accountability in pursuing financial goals and aspirations.
   - **Underdeveloped Leadership Skills**: Without mentorship,

individuals may struggle to develop leadership skills, communication abilities, and emotional intelligence necessary for success in the financial realm and beyond.

7. **Reduced Long-Term Financial Security**:
   - **Impaired Financial Literacy**: Lack of mentorship contributes to impaired financial literacy, limiting individuals' ability to make informed decisions, manage risks, and plan for long-term financial security.
   - **Inadequate Retirement Planning**: Without mentorship, individuals may neglect retirement planning, savings strategies, and investment diversification,

jeopardizing their financial well-being in retirement.

Addressing the lack of mentorship in the financial aspect requires proactive efforts to seek guidance, education, and support from other sources, such as self-directed learning, online resources, financial literacy programs, or peer networks. Building relationships with experienced professionals, seeking mentorship opportunities, and investing in personal development can help individuals overcome the challenges associated with the absence of mentorship and achieve greater financial success and resilience.

Chapter Eleven: Over Confidence

Here's a detailed breakdown of potential outcomes of overconfidentiality in the financial aspect:

1. **Limited Access to Advice and Expertise**:

- **Failure to Seek Guidance**: Overconfidentiality may lead individuals to avoid seeking advice or expertise from financial professionals, mentors, or trusted advisors, fearing that disclosing financial information could compromise their privacy.
- **Missed Opportunities for Insight**: By limiting access to external perspectives and insights, individuals may miss valuable opportunities for learning, growth, and informed decision-making in financial matters.

2. **Inadequate Risk Management**:

- **Lack of Diversification**: Overconfidentiality can hinder individuals from sharing information about their financial goals, risk tolerance, and investment preferences with financial advisors or professionals, resulting in portfolios that lack diversification and expose them to unnecessary risk.

- **Failure to Address Red Flags**: Without external scrutiny or oversight, individuals may overlook potential red flags, warning signs, or market trends that could impact their financial stability or investment performance.

3. **Inefficient Financial Planning**:
   - **Inaccurate Assessments**: Overconfidentiality may lead individuals to provide incomplete or inaccurate information to financial planners, accountants, or tax professionals, resulting in suboptimal financial planning strategies, tax liabilities, or missed opportunities for tax optimization.
   - **Limited Collaboration**: By withholding information or failing to collaborate with financial professionals, individuals may hinder the development of comprehensive financial plans that align with their goals, values, and risk preferences.

4. **Impaired Decision-Making**:
   - **Limited Input**: Overconfidentiality restricts the flow of information and input from trusted advisors, mentors, or peers, depriving individuals of valuable perspectives, feedback, and support in making important financial decisions.
   - **Biased Decision-Making**: Overconfidentiality can lead to biased decision-making, as individuals may rely solely on their own judgment, beliefs, or biases without considering alternative viewpoints or challenging their assumptions.

5. **Risk of Fraud or Scams**:
   - **Vulnerability to Exploitation**: Overconfidentiality may make individuals more susceptible to financial fraud, scams, or exploitation by dishonest individuals who exploit their reluctance to share information or seek external validation.
   - **Inadequate Due Diligence**: Without transparency or verification of financial information, individuals may fail to conduct proper due diligence when evaluating investment opportunities, business ventures, or financial advisors, increasing the risk of falling victim to fraudulent schemes.

6. **Limited Accountability and Oversight**:
   - **Absence of Checks and Balances**: Overconfidentiality can undermine accountability and oversight in financial matters, as individuals may resist sharing information or receiving feedback from trusted sources that could hold them accountable for their financial decisions and actions.
   - **Lack of Performance Monitoring**: Without external scrutiny or accountability mechanisms, individuals may neglect to monitor their financial performance, track progress towards goals, or evaluate the

effectiveness of their financial strategies.

Addressing overconfidentiality in the financial aspect requires individuals to strike a balance between privacy and transparency, recognizing the importance of seeking advice, expertise, and collaboration from trusted professionals, mentors, or advisors. Developing trust, communication skills, and a willingness to share information responsibly can help individuals overcome the barriers associated with overconfidentiality and make more informed, strategic, and resilient financial decisions.

Chapter Twelve: unhealthy Behavior

Here's a detailed breakdown of potential outcomes of unhealthy behavior in the financial aspect:

1. **Excessive Spending**:

- **Impulse Purchases**: Unhealthy financial behavior often involves impulse spending on non-essential items, luxury goods, or experiences without considering the long-term financial consequences.
- **Living Beyond Means**: Individuals may consistently spend more than they earn, relying on credit cards, loans, or borrowing from friends and family to sustain their lifestyle.

2. **Accumulation of Debt**:
   - **Credit Card Debt**: Unhealthy financial behavior can lead to the accumulation of credit card debt, with individuals carrying balances

and paying high interest rates, leading to financial strain and debt cycles.

   - **Loan Defaults**: Failure to manage debt responsibly can result in defaults on loans, such as personal loans, auto loans, or mortgages, leading to damaged credit and financial instability.

3. **Financial Instability**:
   - **Living Paycheck to Paycheck**: Unhealthy financial behavior often results in financial instability, where individuals struggle to cover basic living expenses and lack savings for emergencies or future needs.

- **Risk of Bankruptcy**: Continuous unhealthy financial habits can increase the risk of bankruptcy, as individuals may reach a point where they are unable to repay debts or sustain their lifestyle.

4. **Emotional and Psychological Impact**:
   - **Stress and Anxiety**: Unhealthy financial behavior contributes to stress, anxiety, and worry about financial matters, impacting overall well-being and mental health.
   - **Guilt and Shame**: Individuals may experience feelings of guilt, shame, or inadequacy due to their

financial situation or inability to control spending habits.

5. **Strained Relationships**:
   - **Financial Conflict**: Unhealthy financial behavior can strain personal relationships, marriages, and familial bonds, as partners may disagree on spending habits, financial priorities, or allocation of resources.
   - **Dependency**: Individuals may become financially dependent on others, such as family members or partners, due to their unhealthy financial habits, leading to resentment and conflict in relationships.

6. **Limited Financial Planning**:
   - **Neglect of Savings and Investments**: Unhealthy financial behavior often involves neglecting savings goals, retirement planning, or investment opportunities, leading to a lack of financial security and future uncertainty.
   - **Short-Term Focus**: Individuals may prioritize immediate gratification over long-term financial planning, failing to consider the consequences of their actions on future financial well-being.

7. **Professional Consequences**:
   - **Career Limitations**: Unhealthy financial behavior can

hinder career advancement, job prospects, or professional growth, as financial stress or instability may impact job performance, motivation, or employability.

  - **Financial Misconduct**: Individuals engaged in unhealthy financial behavior may engage in unethical or fraudulent practices in the workplace, risking disciplinary actions, termination, or legal consequences.

Addressing unhealthy behavior in the financial aspect requires individuals to acknowledge and confront their financial habits, attitudes, and beliefs. Developing healthy financial habits, setting realistic goals, seeking support from financial professionals or counselors, and practicing mindfulness and self-discipline are essential steps towards achieving financial stability, well-being, and empowerment.

Chapter Thirteen:

Lack Of Self-confidence

lack of self-confidence in the financial aspect:

1. **Hesitancy to Pursue Opportunities**:
   - **Inaction**: A lack of self-confidence may lead individuals to hesitate or procrastinate when it comes to pursuing financial opportunities such as investing, starting a business, or negotiating a higher salary.
   - **Missed Opportunities**: Inability to take action due to lack of confidence may result in missed opportunities for financial growth, advancement, or wealth accumulation.

2. **Underestimation of Skills and Abilities**:

- **Undervaluing Contributions**: Individuals with low self-confidence may undervalue their skills, knowledge, and expertise in financial matters, leading them to underprice their services or negotiate lower salaries.
  - **Self-Doubt in Decision-Making**: Lack of confidence can result in second-guessing or doubting one's ability to make sound financial decisions, leading to indecision or analysis paralysis.

3. **Fear of Failure**:
   - **Risk Aversion**: Low self-confidence may contribute to risk aversion, as individuals fear

failure or making mistakes in financial endeavors.

  - **Avoidance of Challenges**: Individuals may avoid taking on challenges or pursuing ambitious financial goals due to fear of failure or the perceived inability to handle setbacks.

4. **Ineffective Communication and Advocacy**:
   - **Difficulty Negotiating**: Lack of self-confidence can hinder individuals' ability to negotiate effectively in financial transactions, contracts, or salary negotiations.
   - **Understating Value**: Individuals may struggle to effectively communicate their value

proposition or advocate for themselves in financial matters, resulting in missed opportunities for earning potential or financial rewards.

5. **Limited Networking and Relationship Building**:
   - **Avoidance of Networking**: Individuals with low self-confidence may avoid networking events, industry conferences, or professional gatherings where they can expand their network and build relationships that could lead to financial opportunities.
   - **Difficulty Building Trust**: Lack of confidence may make it challenging for individuals to build

trust and credibility with financial partners, clients, or collaborators, limiting their ability to leverage relationships for financial gain.

6. **Self-Sabotage**:
   - **Negative Self-Talk**: Low self-confidence can lead to negative self-talk and self-sabotaging behaviors that undermine financial success, such as imposter syndrome, self-doubt, or perfectionism.
   - **Setting Unrealistic Expectations**: Individuals may set unrealistic financial goals or expectations for themselves, leading to disappointment, frustration, or burnout when they

are unable to meet these standards.

7. **Stagnation and Limited Growth**:
   - **Lack of Career Advancement**: Individuals with low self-confidence may experience limited career advancement or professional growth opportunities, as they may hesitate to take on new responsibilities or pursue promotions.
   - **Underinvestment in Skills Development**: Lack of confidence may result in underinvestment in skills development, education, or

training necessary for career advancement or financial success.

Addressing lack of self-confidence in the financial aspect requires individuals to work on building self-esteem, self-belief, and assertiveness through self-reflection, personal development, and seeking support from mentors, coaches, or mental health professionals. Developing a growth mindset, setting realistic goals, and celebrating small victories can help individuals overcome self-doubt and take proactive steps towards achieving financial success and empowerment.

Summary:

Beyond the Bank Account: Understanding the Psychological Forces Shaping Financial Success"

In "Beyond the Bank Account," author Abraham Hunter takes readers on a transformative journey into the depths of the human psyche, exploring the intricate interplay of psychological factors that influence financial success. Through a rich tapestry of research, real-life stories, and practical insights, Hunter illuminates the invisible forces that shape our financial behaviors and offers a roadmap for achieving greater financial resilience and empowerment.

At the core of the book lies the recognition that financial success is not solely determined by external factors such as income or investments, but by the complex interplay of beliefs, attitudes, and emotions surrounding money. Drawing from the fields of psychology, economics, and personal finance, Hunter delves into the psychological barriers that hinder financial success, from ingrained attitudes towards money to the cognitive biases that distort our perceptions and decision-making.

One of the central themes explored in the book is the role of self-esteem in financial behavior. Hunter highlights how individuals with low self-esteem may be more prone to impulsive spending and financial insecurity, while those with high self-esteem approach financial decisions with confidence and clarity. By understanding the link between self-esteem and financial behavior, readers are empowered to cultivate a positive self-image and make more informed financial choices.

Moreover, Hunter delves into the pervasive influence of cognitive biases on financial decision-making. From the overconfidence bias that leads us to underestimate risks to the anchoring bias that skews our perceptions of value, these cognitive shortcuts can lead us astray and undermine our financial well-being. By identifying and mitigating these biases, readers can enhance their decision-making processes and avoid common pitfalls in finance.

Throughout the book, Hunter also addresses the profound impact of financial stress on mental health and well-being. He explores how the weight of financial worries can cloud judgment, impair cognitive function, and strain personal relationships, highlighting the urgent need for strategies to manage and alleviate financial stress. Through mindfulness techniques, stress management strategies, and practical financial planning tips, readers learn how to navigate financial challenges with resilience and grace.

Ultimately, "Beyond the Bank Account" offers readers a powerful toolkit for achieving greater financial empowerment and well-being. By understanding the psychological forces at play in financial decision-making, readers can overcome barriers, cultivate healthy financial habits, and chart a course towards a more secure and fulfilling financial future. With its blend of research-based insights, compelling narratives, and actionable advice, this book is a must-read for anyone seeking to master their relationship with money and unlock their full financial potential.

In the latter sections of the book, Hunter delves into practical strategies for applying the insights gained from understanding the psychological forces shaping financial success. Readers are guided through exercises and action steps designed to foster greater self-awareness, improve financial decision-making, and cultivate resilience in the face of financial challenges.

Hunter emphasizes the importance of setting clear financial goals aligned with personal values and aspirations. By articulating their financial vision and priorities, readers can establish a roadmap for their financial journey and make informed decisions that support their long-term objectives.

Furthermore, the book explores the significance of developing healthy financial habits, such as budgeting, saving, and investing wisely. Through mindful spending practices and disciplined money management techniques, readers can take control of their finances and build a solid foundation for future prosperity.

Additionally, Hunter provides guidance on building a support network of mentors, advisors, and peers who can offer guidance, accountability, and encouragement on the path to financial success. By surrounding themselves with positive influences and seeking support when needed, readers can enhance their resilience and stay on track towards their financial goals.

Moreover, "Beyond the Bank Account" addresses the importance of cultivating a growth mindset and embracing failure as a learning opportunity. By reframing setbacks as stepping stones to growth and development, readers can overcome fear and self-doubt and persevere in the face of adversity.

Throughout the book, Hunter emphasizes the transformative power of self-awareness, intentionality, and action in achieving financial empowerment. By harnessing the insights and strategies presented in "Beyond the Bank Account," readers can unlock their full potential, overcome financial obstacles, and create a life of abundance, fulfillment, and prosperity.

In conclusion, "Beyond the Bank Account" is more than just a book about money – it is a guide to mastering the psychological dimensions of financial success. With its blend of cutting-edge research, compelling narratives, and practical advice, this book is destined to become a timeless resource for anyone seeking to transform their relationship with money and create a future of financial freedom and well-being.

www.ingramcontent.com/pod-product-compliance
Lightning Source LLC
Chambersburg PA
CBHW071059240526
45471CB00016B/2169